The Easter STORYBOOK

40 Bible Stories
Showing Who Jesus Is

Laura Richie

Illustrated by Ian Dale

CHASING HOPE | PRESS

DAVID C COOK
transforming lives together

THE EASTER STORYBOOK
Published by David C Cook
4050 Lee Vance Drive
Colorado Springs, CO 80918 U.S.A.

Integrity Music Limited, a Division of David C Cook
Brighton, East Sussex BN1 2RE, England

The graphic circle C logo is a registered trademark of David C Cook.

Library of Congress Control Number 2019944020
ISBN 978-0-8307-7860-7
eISBN 978-0-8307-7861-4

Text © 2020 Laura Richie
Illustrations © 2020 Ian Dale
The Team: Laura Derico, Rachael Stevenson, Nick Lee, Susan Murdock
Cover Design and Illustration: Ian Dale

Printed in India
First Edition 2020

2 3 4 5 6 7 8 9 10 11

092120

To all the little ones who want to see Jesus
(especially Josiah, Grace, Isaiah, and Elisha).
—Laura

To Mom and Dad,
my first picture of God's love.
—Ian

CONTENTS

FROM THE AUTHOR

Dear Reader,

For years, I didn't understand Jesus. I saw God as someone who had a lot of rules I was expected to follow. If I obeyed the rules, I would be rewarded; if I disobeyed, I would be punished. I heard that Jesus had died for my sins so I could have a "relationship" with God, but no one could tell me what that really looked like or why I'd want it. I did want to go to heaven, so I prayed a prayer then began trying hard to be a "good Christian."

I was really good at following the rules. Don't drink, smoke, or do drugs. *Check.* Go to church. *Check.* Read your Bible and pray. *Check.* Save first kiss for wedding day. *Check.* Leave your family and home to follow God (as a missionary kid). *Check.*

Despite my impressive checklist, I had persistent, nagging doubts about being good enough. Two rules seemed extraordinarily difficult: to love God and to love people. How could I love someone who was always watching me then doling out rewards or punishments based on my thoughts and actions? I was trying so hard! But what if I still didn't measure up? And how was I supposed to love all the inconvenient, needy people in my life? They often stood directly in the way of me following the rules well!

One night, I finally confronted the terrifying reality that I could never be good enough, and it brought me to my knees. I cried. I cried hard. I knew in the depths of my being that I would never meet the standard. I could never truly love. All my work was in vain.

And then, for the first time, I saw Jesus.

He knew I couldn't be good enough on my own—that's exactly why He came! I finally understood that He came to rescue me out of my brokenness and into real life.

The Easter Storybook paints a picture of my beautiful Rescuer. Each story adds a stroke to the portrait of the God who came to restore what was broken and find what was lost, the God who promised to send us a Rescuer. The season leading up to Easter, the season of Lent, offers us a special time to pause each day and *remember.* Sit down as a family and remember who Jesus is and why He had to die, then celebrate His victory over evil and death! May you and your family see Jesus and delight in His beauty, love, and grace.

Blessings,

Laura Richie

The Promise
An Introduction

Long ago, God created the world out of nothing.

The Creator made everything good; there was no evil, sadness, or death. The first man and woman lived in a garden full of everything they could ever need. They had perfect friendships with God, with each other, and with all of creation.

But a serpent crept into their beautiful garden, whispering lies. When they believed his lies and defied their good Creator, everything shattered. Their relationship with God and with each other was no longer perfect but broken.

But all was not lost.

God spoke a promise. One day, He would send a Promised Son to crush the head of the serpent and end evil forever. One day, He would come and begin making all things good and new again.

People waited in hope through the dark centuries, longing for the Light. God saw that the people did not know how to love. But God loved His people! So He gave them a way to come close to God and to each other again. The people called this way *korban*, a Hebrew word that means "come close." We call this *sacrifice*.

And God promised that one day a Rescuer would make a way for people to come close to God and each other forever. When this Rescuer, the Promised Son of God, came to earth, no one would need to offer sacrifices again. He would offer the best and perfect sacrifice for everyone.

Then, in the fullness of time, He came!

And that's where our story begins.

The people who walked in darkness
    have seen a great light;
those who dwelt in a land of deep darkness,
    on them has light shone.
You have multiplied the nation;
    you have increased its joy;
they rejoice before you
    as with joy at the harvest,
    as they are glad when they divide the spoil.
For the yoke of his burden,
    and the staff for his shoulder,
    the rod of his oppressor,
    you have broken as on the day of Midian.
For every boot of the tramping warrior in battle tumult
    and every garment rolled in blood
    will be burned as fuel for the fire.
For to us a child is born,
    to us a son is given;
and the government shall be upon his shoulder,
    and his name shall be called
Wonderful Counselor, Mighty God,
    Everlasting Father, Prince of Peace.
Of the increase of his government and of peace
    there will be no end,
on the throne of David and over his kingdom,
    to establish it and to uphold it
with justice and with righteousness
    from this time forth and forevermore.
The zeal of the LORD of hosts will do this.

ISAIAH 9:2–7

Jesus in the Temple
Luke 2

And the Word became flesh and dwelt among us, and we have seen his glory,
glory as of the only Son from the Father, full of grace and truth.
JOHN 1:14

Right from the start, Jesus was not like other little Jewish boys. Angels filled the sky and shepherds praised God when He was born in Bethlehem to a Jewish family—to a young woman, Mary, and her husband, Joseph. Later, wise men traveled to honor the new King of Kings. They all told the good news of the birth of the Messiah—the Savior sent by God to rescue His people.

When Mary took her baby to the Temple for the first time, a prophet of God named Simeon was there. Simeon held the baby in his arms and praised God. "Lord, now I may leave this world in peace, for I have seen your salvation—a light for all people!"

As time passed, Jesus grew strong and was filled with wisdom, and the grace of God was with Him. Like other Jewish families, Jesus and His parents traveled to Jerusalem every year to celebrate Passover, a time to remember when God rescued the Jewish people out of slavery in Egypt.

When the festival ended, Jesus' family and friends all started the long journey home. Suddenly, Mary and Joseph realized Jesus was not with their group. Mary was worried! Jesus was twelve years old, but this wasn't like Him. Mary and Joseph returned to Jerusalem, searching for Jesus. Three days later, they finally found Him. Where was He? Sitting with the teachers in the Temple, listening and asking questions and teaching. Everyone who heard Jesus was amazed at His wisdom and understanding. How could a boy know so much about God and His law?

But Mary was upset. "Son, why have you treated us so? … Your father and I have been searching for you!" (Luke 2:48).

Jesus said, "Why were you looking for me? Didn't you know that I would be here, in my Father's house?" Then the boy, the Son of God, went with His family. It was time to leave the Temple for now, but Jesus would be back.

· ·

Why did Jesus know so much about God? Who was the Messiah?

Beloved Son

Matthew 3; Mark 1; Luke 3; John 1

"You will go before the Lord to prepare his ways, to give knowledge of salvation to his people in the forgiveness of their sins, because of the tender mercy of our God."

LUKE 1:76–78

John, the son of Zechariah, had been born about the same time as Jesus. When he grew up, he became a prophet. Prophets spoke messages from God, and John had a very important message. He told everyone the Messiah was coming to rescue them from their sins.

Many people came to hear John's message, and he baptized those who wanted to be clean and free from their sins, putting them under the waters of the Jordan River and pulling them back up again. John told everyone that people are broken and can't love, but the Messiah was coming to help people love.

Jesus was more than a prophet—He was the Messiah. And when the time was right, Jesus went to see John. John saw Jesus coming and said, "Behold, the Lamb of God, who takes away the sin of the world!" (John 1:29).

John believed.

Jesus asked John to baptize Him. John refused at first, because he knew Jesus was holy—He was all good with no bad. Jesus didn't need to be baptized and cleaned from sin! But Jesus knew God's plan that one day, Jesus would take all of our sin onto Himself. He would die in our place, like a lamb given as a sacrifice. John baptized and cleaned with water, but Jesus would make people new with God's Spirit.

So John baptized Jesus. And when he did, the heavens were opened. John saw God's Spirit come down to rest on Jesus like a dove. And he heard God's voice say, "This is my beloved Son, with whom I am well pleased" (Matthew 3:17).

Jesus, the Promised Son, came to make all things good and new again. He came to heal broken friendships and free us from sin. The Messiah came to help us love God, love each other, and love all of creation—because that's what we were created to do.

· ·

What does sin do? Sin breaks your friendship with God and with others.

Jesus Is Tempted

Matthew 4; Luke 4

The Lord God said to the serpent, "Because you have done this, cursed are you....
I will put enmity between you and the woman, and between your offspring and
her offspring; he shall bruise your head, and you shall bruise his heel."

GENESIS 3:14–15

After Jesus was baptized by John, God's Spirit led Jesus to the desert. Jesus didn't eat for forty days, and He was hungry.

The devil, called Satan, came to tempt Jesus, just as he had tempted Adam and Eve long ago. Adam and Eve believed Satan and disobeyed God, breaking their friendship with God and each other. But God promised to send a Son to crush Satan and end evil forever.

Jesus was that Promised Son. He came to make all things new and good again. Now, the devil didn't want that! So he tried to trick Jesus.

For many years, the Jewish people had been hurt by other nations. The Jews wanted a king who could fight their enemies and set them free. Some thought that the Messiah God had promised to send would be this kind of king. Satan knew this, and he knew Jesus was God's Messiah. But what if Satan could trick Jesus into becoming the king that the people wanted instead?

First, Satan tempted Jesus with food. If Jesus could turn rocks into bread, no one would go hungry, and everyone would know He was the Messiah! But Jesus said no; people who eat bread will still die. For true life, people need the Word of God.

Then Satan tempted Jesus with power. He told Jesus He could become the King over all kingdoms if He did just one thing: worship Satan. But Jesus said no; we should worship only the one true God.

Last, Satan tempted Jesus to test God's faithfulness. He told Jesus to jump off the highest place on the Temple. When God saved Jesus, everyone would know He was the Messiah! But Jesus told the tempter no; God had a different plan.

Jesus stood firm against Satan's lies and obeyed God. Jesus is the true Messiah, and He trusted God and His good plan. Satan left, and angels came to care for Jesus.

. . . .

How was Jesus different from Adam and Eve? Why did the tempter's tricks not work on Jesus?

Jesus Calls Peter
Matthew 4; Luke 5

"My sheep hear my voice, and I know them, and they follow me. I give them eternal life, and they will never perish, and no one will snatch them out of my hand."
JOHN 10:27–28

One morning, a crowd of people followed Jesus to the Sea of Galilee. They were hungry for truth and hope. They wanted to hear Jesus teach.

Peter, a fisherman, was cleaning his nets. He was tired; he had worked all night and caught nothing! Jesus climbed into Peter's boat and asked him to take the boat out a little way. Peter just wanted to go home and sleep, but he gathered up his nets and got back in the boat. Jesus taught the people, and Peter listened too.

When Jesus was done teaching, He told Peter to go out into the deep, deep water and let down the nets again. Peter knew that the best place to catch fish was along the shore, and the best time to catch fish was at night. It didn't make sense to do what Jesus said!

"Teacher," Peter said, "we worked all night and caught nothing. But if you say so, I'll try again." Peter wasn't happy about more work, no fish, and no sleep!

But when Peter let down the nets, he caught *so many* fish that the nets started to break! And when he pulled the fish into the boat, it began to sink!

Peter motioned for his friends James and John to come help. This many fish would sell for a *lot* of money! How did Jesus know about this spot on the lake?

And then Peter stopped. Jesus was teaching people for free when He could be catching all these fish and getting rich! Right then, Peter realized Jesus was special.

Peter fell down at Jesus' knees and said, "Depart from me, for I am a sinful man, O Lord" (Luke 5:8). Peter knew he was a sinner and needed to be rescued.

Before, Peter had caught fish, and the fish had died. Now, Peter would catch people, and the people would get new life! Peter, James, and John decided to follow Jesus.

. . . .

How was Jesus different from anyone else Peter had met?

Jesus Finds the Lost
Luke 15

Surely there is not a righteous man on earth who does good and never sins.
ECCLESIASTES 7:20

Once there were some men who were very angry with Jesus. They were experts in God's law, and they knew Jesus was a friend to people who broke the law. Those "unclean" sinners, like Matthew the tax collector, followed Jesus wherever He went. Jesus even *ate* with sinners, which made Jesus "unclean" too. But the scribes and Pharisees didn't understand that *everyone* breaks the law, and *everyone* needs to have their hearts made clean again. So Jesus told them a story.

A shepherd was out in the wilderness, leading his sheep to grass, still water, and places to rest. It was late in the day, so the shepherd began counting his sheep as he settled them down for the night: "1, 2, 3 … 97, 98, 99?" Oh, no! One sheep was missing!

The shepherd had ninety-nine other sheep, all safe and sound. But he decided to leave them and go look for the one that was missing. He searched everywhere, calling for it. At last, he heard the sheep bleating loudly.

The sheep was found, and the shepherd was so happy! The gentle shepherd carried the scared and worn-out sheep all the way home on his shoulders. He invited his friends to a party so they could all celebrate!

The prophet Isaiah said, "We like sheep have gone astray" (Isaiah 53:6). All of us are broken, lost, and unclean. We all need a Rescuer, just like the lost sheep did.

Jesus, the Good Shepherd, finds the lost and brings us back home to God. He helps us repent. Repenting means knowing you are lost, like the sheep, and reaching out to Jesus. Repenting means knowing you've hurt others and wanting Jesus' help. Repenting is when Jesus finds you and carries you safely home.

The sinners *knew* they were lost like this sheep. Jesus went looking for them and brought them back home, and all of heaven rejoiced!

. . . .

What does it mean to repent?

Jesus Loves the Lost
Luke 15

And he said to him, "Son, you are always with me, and all that is mine is yours. It was fitting to celebrate and be glad, for this your brother was dead, and is alive; he was lost, and is found."

LUKE 15:31–32

Jesus told the Pharisees another story about lost *sons* rather than sheep. Once there was a man who had two sons he loved. The younger son had decided he didn't care about his father or about the family business. He just wanted to sell his share of the land and animals, turn his back on his family, and *leave*.

The father's heart was broken. The whole village watched, and the older son did nothing to stop his brother or help.

The younger son went to a far country. There he wasted all his inheritance, so he had no money left for food. He took a job feeding pigs—an unclean animal to Jews—and wished that he could eat *their* food. He wanted to go home, but if he tried to return, the villagers would have a *Kezazah* ceremony. They would break a pot and say he was cut off from his people forever.

But he had no choice; he was starving. He decided to go home and beg to be a servant, because his father's servants always had plenty to eat.

As he got close, he was shocked to see his father *running* toward him. Men where he lived *never* ran. And his father didn't even look angry. He looked happy! As his father's arms wrapped around him, the son finally realized how much his father loved him.

The father invited everyone to celebrate. He replaced his son's rags with a fine robe, a ring, and shoes to show he was a *son* again, not a servant. Since the father showed such love, the villagers welcomed the son home too.

But the older son was angry. He insulted his father by refusing to go to the party. His father had accepted his brother, a sinner. It was completely unfair!

The father should have been angry with his older son, but he showed compassion again. "Son, all I have is yours—but let's celebrate, because your brother was lost and is now found!"

. . . .

How is Jesus like the father in this story?

Jesus Feeds His Sheep
Matthew 14; Mark 6; Luke 9

When he went ashore he saw a great crowd, and he had compassion on them, because they were like sheep without a shepherd. And he began to teach them many things.

MARK 6:34

It was time to send out Jesus' disciples! Jesus wanted them to do good things: heal the sick, cast out bad spirits, and tell everyone that their sins could be forgiven. Jesus sent them out in pairs; together they could help the Promised Son make everything good and new again.

But while they were gone, something terrible happened.

A Roman king named Herod had a big party for all the important, powerful people. To show off his power and to impress his guests, Herod ordered someone to kill the prophet John, the one who had baptized Jesus. John was part of Jesus' family. When the Jewish people heard that John had been killed, they were very angry and sad.

Jesus' friends hurried back to Jesus when they heard the sad news. People crowded around Jesus and His friends. They wished Jesus was their king instead of Herod! However, Jesus didn't come to be a king like that.

Jesus told His friends to come away on the sea and rest. But the people followed them. When their boat reached shore, Jesus and His disciples couldn't rest because a great crowd was already there. But Jesus loved them. He saw that they were like sheep without a shepherd, and He wanted to help. He taught them and healed them.

It was getting late, and everyone was hungry. Jesus told the disciples, "You give them something to eat" (Mark 6:37). His friends were shocked. How could they feed this many people? They only had five loaves of bread and two fish!

Jesus told the people to sit on the grass. Then Jesus looked up to heaven, spoke a blessing, broke the loaves, and gave the loaves and fish to His disciples. His friends gave the food to everyone, and they were all full! There were even twelve baskets of food left over! The disciples couldn't feed more than five thousand hungry people—but Jesus could.

· ·

How did Jesus, the Good Shepherd, care for these people?

Jesus Walks on Water
Matthew 14; Mark 6; John 6

Even though I walk through the valley of the shadow of death, I will fear no evil, for you are with me; your rod and your staff, they comfort me.

PSALM 23:4

When Jesus fed five thousand hungry people in the wilderness, everyone was excited! Herod, the bad king, had a party that ended in death. Jesus, the King of Kings, provided a banquet that gave life.

After the people had eaten, Jesus told His disciples to go ahead of Him in a boat to the other shore. Then He told the crowds to go home. Jesus was alone. He went up the mountain to pray.

By this time, the boat was a long way from land and the wind and waves were pushing against it. Sometime before dawn, the disciples saw something coming toward them, walking on the water. *Was it a ghost?* Jesus' friends were terrified! Then the figure said, "Take heart; it is I. Do not be afraid" (Matthew 14:27).

It was Jesus!

Peter said, "Lord, if it is you, tell me to come to you on the water."

"Come," Jesus said. Peter got out of the boat and walked toward Jesus *on the water*! But when Peter saw the wind and waves, he began to sink. Peter was afraid and cried out, "Lord, save me!" And Jesus reached out and saved him. When Jesus and Peter climbed into the boat, the wind stopped, and the disciples were amazed.

Jesus had healed people, fed them, and forgiven them. Jesus was doing the same good things God had done for His people since the beginning of the world. Peter and the other disciples saw that Jesus was special. They began to understand that Jesus was the Messiah, God's Promised Son. "And those in the boat worshiped him, saying, 'Truly you are the Son of God'" (v. 33).

. . . .

Have you ever felt afraid? Who can protect you?

Jesus Teaches
Matthew 5–6; Luke 6, 12

"Fear not, little flock, for it is your Father's good pleasure to give you the kingdom."
LUKE 12:32

Jesus often taught people about His kingdom. One time, He hiked up a mountain, and a great crowd gathered around Him. Messages from God had come to the people from mountains many times in the past. Jesus looked in their eyes and saw that they wanted wisdom and hope. Then Jesus told them what life would be like when He was King, and everything was good and new again.

Jesus taught that things are different in His kingdom. People love God and each other. No one gets into this kingdom by working hard or paying lots of money. The strong and proud do not rule this kingdom either.

Instead, those who live humble lives will be happy and free there. Those who are sad will find comfort. Those who seek goodness will find God's perfect holiness. People will be kind and merciful and live in peace. And they will be happy!

Do you ever worry? The people Jesus was teaching had many worries—what to eat, what to drink, and what to wear. Some of them were very poor.

Jesus saw the worry lines on their faces. But He looked past the crowds to the lovely lilies growing on the hillside. He glanced up at the sky and saw birds in graceful flight. Then Jesus told the crowd, "Birds do no work at all, and God cares for them. Lazy lilies do not spin wool for their robes, and God makes them beautiful. Don't worry!" The people smiled and felt safe. Jesus said, "God knows just what you need. If He cares so much for every bird and blade of grass, how much more do you think He cares for you?"

Then Jesus gave this promise: "Seek first the kingdom of God and his righteousness, and all these things will be added to you" (Matthew 6:33).

In His kingdom, we have everything we need! God wants us to be in His kingdom. That's why He sent Jesus.

. . . .

What do you worry about? How can you remember what Jesus says about worrying?

Jesus Calms the Storm
Matthew 8; Mark 4; Luke 8

Who is mighty as you are, O LORD, with your faithfulness all around you?
You rule the raging of the sea; when its waves rise, you still them.
PSALM 89:8–9

One day, Jesus and His disciples decided to cross the Sea of Galilee. They climbed into a boat and set sail, and Jesus fell asleep. Peter, James, and John were all fishermen and knew how to handle a boat. They didn't need Jesus' help.

But while they were sailing, a great storm arose. Fierce winds pushed against the water and giant waves formed.

When water began pouring into the boat and they knew that they were about to drown, the disciples cried out to Jesus, "Master, Master, we are perishing!" (Luke 8:24).

Jesus woke up and told the fierce winds and giant waves to *stop.*

What do you think happened?

The wind and waves stopped, just like that!

Everything was still.

The disciples were amazed. They had traveled on this sea many times. They had seen boats destroyed by such a storm. And they knew there was nothing they could do to stop a storm like that.

But Jesus could. Jesus—this man who was their teacher and friend. They had walked dusty roads and eaten simple meals together. They had seen Jesus be kind and sad, hungry and tired. But now they saw Him again—powerful and strong and fully in charge.

That storm was too strong for Peter, James, and John.

But it wasn't too strong for Jesus.

The disciples asked, "What sort of man is this, that even winds and sea obey him?" (Matthew 8:27).

. . . .

What sort of person do you think Jesus is?

Jesus Casts Out Demons
Matthew 8; Mark 5; Luke 8

*For freedom Christ has set us free; stand firm therefore, and
do not submit again to a yoke of slavery.*
GALATIANS 5:1

Jesus and His friends sailed across the Sea of Galilee to where the Gerasenes lived. The Gerasenes were Gentiles—people who were not Jews.

A Gerasene man saw Jesus step off the boat. The man was naked and lived in the tombs among the dead. He often hurt others, so people tried to put chains on him. But the man was suffering with a mind and body full of demons—evil spirits. The demons made him so strong and wild that he would break the chains!

Jesus saw what was wrong with the man. He told the demons to come out. He wanted the man to be free!

The demons in the man cried out, "What are you doing, Jesus, Son of the Most High God? Please don't torment us!" The demons thought that if they knew Jesus' name, He wouldn't be able to control them. But they were *wrong*.

The demons begged Jesus to send them into a herd of pigs. In that world, pigs were one of the most unclean animals—they would eat anything, even trash! Jewish people stayed far away from pigs. So Jesus told the unclean spirits to leave the man and go into the unclean pigs. When they did, all the pigs madly ran down the hill and drowned, taking the demons with them.

Jesus and His disciples found clothes for the man. He sat down at Jesus' feet, listening to Him. The man was so thankful to be healed and set free!

The Gerasenes heard what happened. They wondered, *Who was this man who could send a whole herd of pigs into the sea? Who was this man who could make evil spirits obey?* They saw how strong and good Jesus was, but they asked Him to leave. The loss of all the pigs was costly, and they were afraid of what else this Jesus might do.

The man, free from demons, went back to his family and friends, telling everyone how Jesus had rescued him!

. . . .

What does it mean to be free? Freedom means being able to do what you were created to do.

Jesus Offers Grace

John 7–8

"Come, everyone who thirsts, come to the waters; and he who has no money, come, buy and eat! Come, buy wine and milk without money and without price."
ISAIAH 55:1

Jesus once sat down at the Temple to teach. At this time, the religious leaders were very angry at Jesus. Jesus had told everyone that He was God—the One who gives living water to the thirsty. But the Pharisees didn't believe Jesus. So they decided to set a trap to make Jesus look bad.

While Jesus was teaching, the religious leaders dragged a woman in front of the crowd. They announced to everyone that she was a bad sinner. According to their law, the woman should be stoned to death. "So what do *you* say, Jesus?"

This was their trap. If Jesus agreed that the woman should be killed, the Roman guards would arrest Him for causing trouble. But if Jesus said that the Jewish law didn't matter, the crowds would stop listening to Him.

What would Jesus say?

While the people waited to hear His answer, Jesus bent down and wrote in the dirt. Then Jesus stood and said, "Let him who is without sin among you be the first to throw a stone at her" (John 8:7). Jesus bent down and began writing again.

Yes, the sinful woman had broken God's laws. But she wasn't the only one! No person in the crowd was without sin. They *all* deserved punishment.

One by one, each person walked away.

Jesus knew that God's law was all about *love*. Jesus loved this woman and rescued her. He showed her grace.

When everyone left, Jesus looked at the woman. "Where are they? Has anyone condemned you?"

She looked at her Rescuer and said, "No one, Lord" (v. 11).

Then Jesus, the only One who was without sin, said, "Neither do I condemn you; go, and from now on sin no more" (v. 11). He gave the woman a new life, a second chance.

. . . .

How do you think this woman felt about Jesus, her Rescuer?

Jesus Shows Who Is Righteous
Luke 18

The sacrifices of God are a broken spirit; a broken and contrite heart, O God, you will not despise.
PSALM 51:17

Once, Jesus wanted to teach people what it means to be righteous. He told a story about two very different men. One man was a Pharisee, and the other man was a tax collector.

Both men went to the Temple to pray. It was time for the atonement service, when a lamb was killed as a sacrifice for Israel's sins, bringing people close to God and to each other again.

The Pharisee stood apart from everyone else, because he didn't want an "unclean" person to touch him. He prayed, "God, I thank you that *I* am not like other men who sin, especially like this tax collector. I obey your laws extra well—unlike other people, I fast two times *every week*, and I tithe from *everything* I own."

This Pharisee was very proud of himself! He just *knew* that he was righteous, because he followed the rules better than almost anyone!

The tax collector also stood far off. But he was so sad about his sins that he beat his chest and didn't look up at heaven. He prayed, "God, have mercy on me. I'm a sinner!"

The tax collector *knew* he had done bad things. He couldn't love God or others on his own. He knew that the lamb in the Temple was dying for *his* sins. He knew he could never be righteous—able to love God, others, and all of creation—on his own.

Then Jesus said something surprising. "This tax collector was made righteous, but the Pharisee was not." The Pharisee was too proud to ask for forgiveness. He thought he could be good enough all by himself.

God wants us all to be righteous, but we can't do that on our own. We need Jesus! One day, Jesus would become like the lamb in the Temple; He would die in our place because of our sins. And when the Lamb of God did that, He made people righteous—able to love God and each other and all of creation forever!

. . . .

How was the tax collector different from the Pharisee?

Jesus Is Loved Much
Luke 7

"Repent, for the kingdom of heaven is at hand."
MATTHEW 3:2

One day, a Pharisee named Simon invited Jesus for a meal. Eating with someone usually meant you were friends. But when Jesus entered, no one kissed His cheek to greet Him. No one washed His dusty feet and hands. No one anointed His head with oil.

People at that time greeted their guests this way. But not Simon! Simon didn't want to be Jesus' friend. He wanted to hurt Jesus' feelings.

Everyone was watching. One of the women there came and stood behind Jesus. She was known in the city as a sinner. And now here she was, in the Pharisee's house, holding an expensive jar of perfumed ointment and weeping.

She had heard Jesus teach. She knew that He came to rescue everyone, even sinners like her. She believed Jesus was her Rescuer, and she wanted to honor Him and love Him.

She had been treated badly by people like Simon before. Now she saw Jesus being treated badly. The woman knelt and washed Jesus' feet with her tears. She dried them with her hair. She kissed His feet. Finally, she anointed His feet with the precious perfume.

No one could believe it! Simon muttered, "If Jesus was a *real* prophet, He would know what a bad sinner this woman is. He shouldn't let *her* touch Him!"

But Jesus knew what Simon was thinking. So He told one of His teaching stories.

Two people owed money to a man. One person owed a *lot*—500 denarii! The other person owed a *little*—50 denarii. But neither could pay back the money. What did the man do? He said that they didn't have to pay back *any* money! He forgave them.

Jesus asked Simon, "Which person will love the man the most?"

Simon said, "I guess, the one who owed the most?"

"Right!" Jesus said. "I forgive this woman's many sins, and she loves much. But those who think they have few sins are forgiven little and, like you, love little."

. . . .

Why did the woman love Jesus? Why did Simon not love Jesus?

Jesus and the Rich Man
Matthew 19; Mark 10; Luke 18

For all have sinned and fall short of the glory of God, and are justified by his grace as a gift.
ROMANS 3:23–24

One man always tried very hard to follow all the rules. He wanted to be good enough so he could earn life that lasts forever. This man walked up to Jesus and asked, "Good Teacher, what good things must I do to get eternal life?"

Jesus said that only God is good. Jesus reminded the man of God's laws: be loyal to your family, don't kill, don't steal, and tell the truth. The man was delighted! He was *sure* he had followed all of those rules since he was just a boy.

Then Jesus said, "There is one more thing. Sell everything you have, give the money to the poor, and then come and follow me."

The man was crushed. Sell *everything*? He was very rich and had so much to take care of! His family had owned their land for generations! Now he must leave his family and home to follow Jesus? Who would take care of his parents? It was too hard.

The people listening agreed. "Do all of *that*? That's impossible!"

Jesus said, "It is easier for a camel to go through the eye of a needle than for a rich person to enter the kingdom of God" (Luke 18:25).

People at that time knew that rich men were able to do more good deeds than anyone else. The people asked, "If rich men can't enter heaven—with all of their good works—then who can?"

Jesus replied, "What is impossible with man is possible with God" (v. 27).

Peter pointed out, "Like us! You helped us, and we left everything to follow You!"

Jesus said, "That's right. Those who are willing to leave what matters most on this earth will receive much more now. And they will receive life with God that lasts forever!"

Jesus rescues us. He makes us true friends with Him and with others. He helps us love and gives us true life, both now and forever.

· ·

What is impossible with humans but possible with God?

Jesus and the Children
Matthew 18–19; Mark 10; Luke 18

*How precious is your steadfast love, O God! The children of
mankind take refuge in the shadow of your wings.*

PSALM 36:7

As they were traveling in Galilee, Jesus' friends asked Him a question: "Who is the greatest in the kingdom of heaven?" (Matthew 18:1).

The kingdom of heaven is wherever God is King and everything is good. Jesus' friends thought that maybe people with a lot of money would be the most important people in the kingdom. Or maybe those who prayed or fasted the most would be the greatest.

Jesus called over a child. Now in that time no one asked children for their thoughts. No one gave children special treatment. But Jesus said, "Whoever humbles himself like this child is the greatest in the kingdom of heaven" (v. 4).

Children don't have a lot of money. They don't have power. They don't pray or fast to be the best. They just love Jesus.

In God's kingdom, the people who realize their need for Jesus will be great. People who are like little children—who seem unimportant to everyone else—are very special to Jesus.

At another time, parents were bringing their children, even tiny babies, to Jesus. Jewish mothers and fathers usually brought their children to the Temple to receive blessings from the priest. But these parents wanted *Jesus* to bless their children.

The disciples held back the parents. Perhaps they thought Jesus was too busy to see the children. So many people wanted to hear Jesus and be healed by Him!

But Jesus showed the disciples again that they did not understand. "Let the little children come! Don't stop them! The kingdom of God belongs to those who have the faith of children." And Jesus took the little ones in His arms. He blessed all the children and prayed for them, and then sent them back to their happy parents.

. . . .

Why is it good to be like a child?

The Good Samaritan

Luke 10

In this the love of God was made manifest among us, that God sent his only Son into the world, so that we might live through him.

1 JOHN 4:9

As Jesus was talking with His disciples, an expert in the law came to test Jesus with this question: "How can I live forever?"

Jesus asked the man what the law commanded. The man knew *that* answer: "Love the Lord your God with all your heart, soul, strength, and mind. And love your neighbor as yourself." And then he asked Jesus, "Who is my neighbor?"

The expert thought he could find out who to love, check that off his list, and get eternal life. But then Jesus told this story.

On the long road from Jerusalem to Jericho, robbers attacked a Jewish traveler. They beat him until he almost died. They took everything, even the man's clothes!

A wealthy priest came along and saw the man. But the priest could not tell whether the poor man was sick or dead. He did not want to touch him and become "unclean" and unable to serve in the Temple. So the priest passed by as far away as he could.

A Levite, a helper to the priests, also traveled on that road. But the Levite knew the same laws as the priest and did not want to touch the man. So the healthy helper walked right on past the hurting person.

The next traveler was a Samaritan. Jews *hated* Samaritans. They lived in separate places and tried to avoid each other. But this Samaritan chose to love the hurting man. He went to the bruised man and bandaged his wounds. Then the Samaritan put the man on his own donkey and took him to an inn in Jericho. When he left the next day, he gave his own money to the innkeeper to care for the man.

Jesus asked, "Which of these three was a good neighbor?"

The expert answered, "The one who showed mercy."

The Samaritan man truly loved his neighbor. He gave the hurt man what he needed, even when it was hard. The good Samaritan was like Jesus. Jesus shows us true love.

. . . .

What is love? Love is wanting good for someone and then doing that good, even when it's hard.

The Son of Man Shines

Matthew 16–17; Mark 9; Luke 9

"Father, I desire that they also, whom you have given me, may be with me where I am, to see my glory that you have given me because you loved me before the foundation of the world."

JOHN 17:24

When Jesus lived on the earth, many people tried to understand who He was. Once, Jesus asked His close friends, "What are people saying about me?" Some people thought He was John the Baptist or Elijah or another prophet. Then Jesus asked His friends, "'But who do you say that I am?' Simon Peter replied, 'You are the Christ, the Son of the living God'" (Matthew 16:15–16).

A few days later, Jesus took Peter, James, and John up onto a high mountain to pray. The disciples tried to pray, but they were too sleepy. But as Jesus was praying, His face began to shine with glory like the sun, and His clothes became bright white! Then two men appeared and talked with Jesus. They were Moses and Elijah, important prophets from long, long ago!

The disciples were amazed, and Peter tried to say something helpful. He was offering to give each man a tent when something *else* happened! A bright cloud overshadowed them, and God's voice spoke: "This is my beloved Son, with whom I am well pleased; listen to him" (17:5).

Peter, James, and John fell on their faces and were terrified. They were *with God* in all His goodness and power and glory, and it was too much for them.

But Jesus said, "Rise, and have no fear" (v. 7). And then they saw only Jesus, Son of God and Son of Man. For just a little bit, they had seen His true glory and light. Through Jesus, God had come to live with broken people. But why?

Jesus came to bring people close to God and to each other again. He would suffer and die, but on the third day He would come back to life! Jesus told Peter, James, and John, "Tell no one the vision, until the Son of Man is raised from the dead" (v. 9).

Jesus' friends still didn't understand everything. But Jesus would help them.

. . . .

What do you think it was like to see Jesus' glory and to hear God's voice?

Jesus Gives Sight
John 9

"One thing I do know, that though I was blind, now I see."
JOHN 9:25

Once, there was a man who had always been blind. He had never seen his mom smile. He had never seen golden sunlight sparkle on blue water. He had never seen anything at all.

Because he was blind, he couldn't work as other men did at that time. He had to ask for money and help.

One day, the man heard people nearby talking about him. They were wondering whether he was blind because of his sin or the sin of his parents.

Then another man's voice answered, "No sin caused this. But the works of God can now be displayed in him." The man went on to say, "I am the light of the world" (John 9:5).

The blind man then heard someone spit on the ground. And he felt fingers on his closed eyes, gently wiping mud on them. Then that voice spoke again: "Go, wash in the pool of Siloam" (v. 7).

He went and washed and … he could *see!* He hurried back to find the man who had done this amazing thing—to find Jesus. And everyone who knew him as a blind man was amazed. They kept asking, "Isn't this the man who used to beg for money?"

But the Pharisees were not amazed or happy. They were angry that this work of healing was done on the Sabbath, the day of rest. They declared that Jesus was a sinner because He worked on the Sabbath.

But the man who had been blind said, "No one has ever been able to give sight to a man who was born blind. If this Jesus were not from God, He could do nothing."

The Pharisees were so angry that they told the man he could no longer worship with his family or friends. They cast him out. But Jesus found the man, and the man worshipped Jesus. He said, "Lord, I believe" (v. 38). Jesus helped the man's eyes see, and Jesus helped his heart see too.

How did Jesus change this man's life?

Lord of the Sabbath
Matthew 12; Mark 2–3; Luke 6

*"You shall love the Lord your God with all your heart and with all your
soul and with all your mind. This is the great and first commandment.
And a second is like it: You shall love your neighbor as yourself."*
MATTHEW 22:37–39

Do you have rules at your house, like "Be kind" or "Don't hit"? Good rules show us what is right and good to do. But sometimes people make rules that are unwise, hard to follow, and might even hurt people. We shouldn't obey bad rules.

You have heard of the rule-loving Pharisees, who lived at the time of Jesus. They had so many rules they had added to the law of God! They had many rules about exactly what Jewish people could or could not do on the Sabbath, the day of rest.

Jesus and His friends were walking through some fields on the Sabbath. They were hungry, so they picked grain and ate it. But the Pharisees were watching. They let Jesus know that His followers were breaking the rules! God had told people long ago to *rest* on the Sabbath, not *work*! And picking grain was work!

Now, Jesus knew all about the Sabbath. He knew *why* God had created this day of rest. The most important thing was how the Sabbath reminded people about God. No matter how hard we work, it's still God who gives us what we need. And no matter how hard we try, we won't be good enough on our own. It's God who helps us do good and love well.

Jesus told the Pharisees, "The Sabbath was made for man, not man for the Sabbath. So the Son of Man is lord even of the Sabbath" (Mark 2:27–28). Jesus was saying He was in charge!

Later, Jesus went into a place of worship on the Sabbath and saw a man with a withered right hand. The man couldn't use his hand at all. Jesus said, "Stretch it out." And when the man stretched out his hand, it was healed! Jesus made it good and new again!

The Pharisees were angry yet again. But Jesus knew that the most important rule was to love. And that's what He did—Sabbath or not.

. . . .

Why did Jesus heal people on the Sabbath?

Rise and Walk
Matthew 9; Mark 2; Luke 5

"The blind receive their sight and the lame walk, lepers are cleansed and the deaf hear, and the dead are raised up, and the poor have good news preached to them. And blessed is the one who is not offended by me."

MATTHEW 11:5–6

People loved to be around Jesus. He told the truth, gave hope, and healed people. One day, Jesus was teaching in a house in Capernaum. There were so many people inside that no one else could fit! A man who couldn't walk heard that Jesus was in town, and four of his friends carried him to Jesus. The man wanted to be healed! But there were too many people in the way.

The four men saw the crowd and decided to make a way to Jesus … through the roof! They walked up the steps on the side of the house, carrying the paralyzed man on his mat. Then they dug through the mud and branches of the roof and lowered their friend to the ground in front of Jesus.

Jesus saw the man's hope to be healed. Jesus saw the determination of the man's friends. Jesus knew they believed.

When Jesus saw their faith, He said, "Son, your sins are forgiven" (Mark 2:5).

The man had been taught his whole life that he couldn't walk because of his sins. But could Jesus really forgive his sins and make him new? Some scribes heard Jesus, and they thought to themselves, *He can't say that! Only God can forgive sins!* The scribes didn't believe that Jesus was the Messiah.

Jesus knew what they were thinking. "Why do you question this?" He asked. "Which is easier, to say 'Your sins are forgiven,' or to say, 'Rise, take your bed, and walk'? I want you to know that the Son of Man has the power on earth to forgive sins."

And then Jesus looked at the paralyzed man and said, "Rise, pick up your bed, and go home" (v. 11).

And the man could walk! He was healed right then!

Everyone who saw this miracle was amazed and praised God. Jesus was making all things new, forgiving sins and fixing what was broken.

. . . .

What do you think was the first thing the man did when he could walk?

The Soldier's Faith

Matthew 8; Luke 7

Now faith is the assurance of things hoped for, the conviction of things not seen.
HEBREWS 11:1

Once, there was a Roman centurion, a soldier, who was very worried about his servant. These soldiers weren't supposed to get married until they were finished with their work, so sometimes their servants were the only family they had. When the soldier heard about Jesus, he suddenly had hope. Maybe Jesus could heal this servant the soldier loved!

The centurion was a friend to some of the Jewish leaders, even though he was not Jewish, and he thought that Jesus would listen to them. He asked his Jewish friends to ask Jesus to heal his servant. The leaders told Jesus, "The centurion deserves this. He loves the Jewish people, and he spent a lot of money building our synagogue."

Jesus went with the leaders, and when He had almost reached the soldier's "unclean" house, some of the soldier's friends came outside to give Jesus a message.

The centurion's message was this: "Lord, don't worry about coming into my house. I don't deserve that honor. Just say the word, and I know my servant will be healed. I am in charge of many soldiers; they do whatever I say. I know you have great power too. I believe you can heal people by simply commanding it to happen."

This Roman centurion believed in Jesus!

Jesus was amazed at the man's belief. He looked at the crowd around Him and said, "I tell you, not even in Israel have I found such faith" (Luke 7:9).

Then Jesus made the dying servant well, right then and there, without even stepping into the house. Jesus just spoke and healing happened!

Jesus came to make all things good and new, not only for Jewish people but for *all* people. He rescues all who believe—all who realize their need for Him.

. . . .

The centurion had great faith. What do you believe Jesus can do?

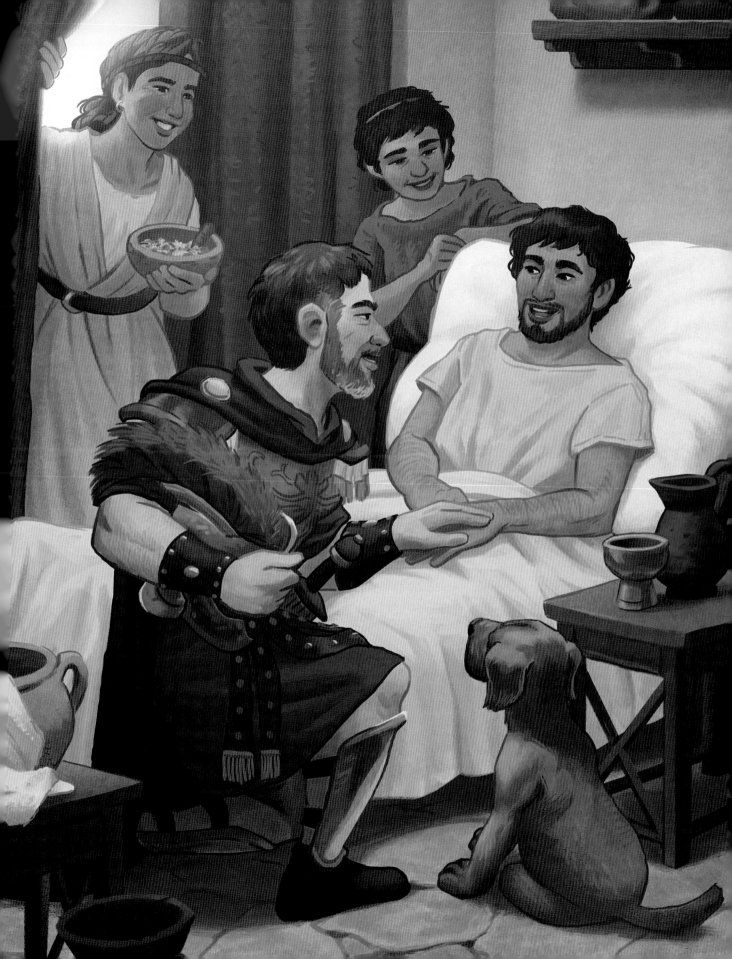

Jesus Gives Life

Matthew 9; Mark 5; Luke 8

"For as the Father raises the dead and gives them life, so also the Son gives life to whom he will."

JOHN 5:21

One day, an important Jewish leader named Jairus came up to Jesus and fell at His feet. The man's heart was breaking, because his only daughter was about to die. He knew that Jesus was her only hope. He begged Jesus to come heal her. Jesus agreed and began walking with him, and a great crowd of people followed.

Suddenly, Jesus stopped and said, "Who touched me?"

Peter reminded Jesus that a *lot* of people were touching Him—the crowd was all around. But Jesus said, "Someone touched me because power has gone out from me."

And then a trembling woman came forward. She had been bleeding for twelve years, and no one had been able to heal her. Because of her illness, she was considered "unclean" by the Jewish leaders. She couldn't touch anyone or be touched, because she would make them "unclean" too. But when the suffering woman saw Jesus, she knew that just touching the edge of His robe would heal her. The woman believed in Jesus' power!

And she was right. The moment she touched Jesus' clothing, her bleeding stopped! Jesus said to her, "Daughter, your faith has made you well; go in peace" (Luke 8:48).

Right then, someone came to Jairus and said, "Your daughter is dead" (v. 49). Oh, no! They were too late!

Jesus said, "Do not fear; only believe, and she will be well" (v. 50). When they arrived at the house, everyone was crying and mourning for her. "Don't cry," Jesus said, "she is just sleeping." Everyone laughed at this. They didn't believe Jesus.

As soon as Jesus took the twelve-year-old girl's hand, she got up—alive again! Jesus healed her! Jairus and his wife were amazed at Jesus' goodness and power.

Jesus gave new life to the bleeding woman and life to the dead little girl. Jesus came to give all of us new life too!

. . . .

How is the healing Jesus does different from what a doctor can do?

Life for Lazarus
John 11

"The dead will hear the voice of the Son of God, and those who hear will live."
JOHN 5:25

Lazarus, a friend of Jesus, was very sick. Lazarus lived in Judea, and the Jewish leaders in Judea were angry with Jesus. They wanted to kill Him. But Mary and Martha, sisters of Lazarus, asked Jesus to come. They knew their brother was about to die.

Jesus told His friends, "This sickness is for God, so that people may see the glory of the Son of God. Lazarus has fallen asleep, but I will awaken him."

The disciples decided to go with Jesus to Judea even though it was dangerous. Thomas said, "Let us also go, that we may die with him" (John 11:16).

When Jesus arrived, Lazarus had been dead and in the tomb for four days. Martha went out to meet Jesus and said, "Lord, if you had been here, my brother would not have died. But even now I know that whatever you ask from God, God will give you" (vv. 21–22).

Jesus said, "I am the resurrection and the life. Whoever believes in me, though he die, yet shall he live, and everyone who lives and believes in me shall never die. Do you believe this?" (vv. 25–26). Whoever believes in Jesus has true life!

Martha answered, "Yes, Lord; I believe that you are the Christ, the Son of God" (v. 27).

Then Mary came to where Jesus was. And many others who were crying about the death of their friend came with her. Jesus was greatly troubled by their tears and pain and sorrow. Do you know what Jesus did? Jesus cried too!

Then they took Jesus to the tomb, and He told them to roll away the stone at the entrance. Jesus prayed to His Father and cried out in a loud voice, "Lazarus, come out!"

And Lazarus, the dead man, came back to life! He walked out of the cave, with the burial cloths still wrapped around him.

Jesus brought life out of death! Soon, Jesus would conquer death forever.

Many who saw this miracle believed in Jesus, the Son of God. He gives life to all who believe that He is their Rescuer.

. . . .

Who can give us true life?

Jesus Talks with Nicodemus
John 3

"You shall be clean from all your uncleanness.… I will give you a new heart, and a new spirit.… I will put my Spirit within you."
EZEKIEL 36:25–27

Not all the Pharisees were angry with Jesus. Nicodemus was a Pharisee who saw the good things Jesus did and taught. He wondered, *Could this be the Messiah, the one God is sending to bring His kingdom?* Nicodemus knew his friends would be angry if they saw him talking with Jesus, so he went to Jesus at night. He said, "Rabbi, we know that you are a teacher come from God" (John 3:2).

Jesus understood that Nicodemus wanted to know how to be in God's kingdom. "You have to be born again to see the kingdom of God," Jesus said.

Nicodemus was confused. "How can a man be born when he is old? He's too big to be a baby in his mother's womb again!"

Jesus explained, "Truly, unless one is born of water *and* the Spirit, he can't be a part of God's kingdom. Being born of the flesh makes you human. But being born of the Spirit gives you true life. Consider how the wind blows and you can hear it, but you can't see where it comes from or where it goes. This is how it is for everyone who is born of the Spirit. The Spirit of God lives in them, helping them to know God and believe. You can't see where the wind is from, but you can see what it does."

"How can this be?" Nicodemus couldn't believe it. For years he had believed that working hard to follow God's rules was the way to enter God's kingdom.

Jesus had been *with* God; He had seen true life in God's kingdom. Jesus told Nicodemus, "God loves the world so much, He sent His only Son, so that whoever believes in Him will not die but have eternal life."

Jesus said people needed *new life*. It wasn't enough to be clean on the outside—they needed new hearts that could love and be loved. New life came from believing Jesus. God's Spirit comes to be with those who believe, giving them new life.

. . . .

How does Jesus give us new life?

Living Water
John 4

They said to the woman, "It is no longer because of what you said that we believe, for we have heard for ourselves, and we know that this is indeed the Savior of the world."
JOHN 4:42

Jesus and His disciples were walking through where the Samaritans lived—people who were not friends with the Jews. Most Jews walked *around* Samaria, but not Jesus. He was tired and sat down near a well in a Samaritan town while His friends went to buy food.

It was around noon when a Samaritan woman came to the well. Every day, she had to fill up a big jar with water and carry it home. Women usually went together in the cool of the morning to get water—but not this woman. She came by herself when the sun was hot.

She saw Jesus but walked up anyway, even though men didn't talk to women in public then. Jesus was thirsty. He saw the leather bucket she carried and asked her for a drink. The woman said she couldn't believe a Jewish man was not only *talking* to her, but also willing to drink out of her "unclean" bucket!

Jesus answered, "If you knew who was talking to you, you would ask, and He would give you living water."

The woman didn't understand. "Where do you get that living water?" (John 4:11).

"Whoever drinks the water I give will never be thirsty again. This spring of water will live inside the person, giving eternal life," Jesus said. Then He told the woman about her sin. He knew why she came to the well all alone. The woman was nervous. Would this prophet still give her living water and true life, even though she was a bad sinner?

She mentioned something Jews and Samaritans disagreed about. Then she said, "I know the Messiah will come and explain all this to us in time."

Jesus answered, "I am the Messiah."

The woman believed! She returned to town and told everyone about Jesus—how He knew everything she had done and still offered her living water and new life. And many others in that town came to hear Jesus and believed Him too.

. . . .

What does it mean to believe? Believing means thinking something is true and then living like it is true.

Jesus Loves Zacchaeus
Luke 19

*For by grace you have been saved through faith. And this is not your own doing;
it is the gift of God, not a result of works, so that no one may boast.*
EPHESIANS 2:8–9

As Jesus traveled to Jerusalem, He passed through Jericho. In Jericho lived a man named Zacchaeus, who wanted to see Jesus. But Zacchaeus had problems. Not only was he short, but he was also a tax collector. A *rich* tax collector, which meant he had cheated his neighbors and kept their money for himself. Everyone *hated* Zacchaeus. He knew it wasn't safe to be out in the crowd, and he couldn't see over all the people who were waiting for Jesus to pass by, so he decided to do something no one would expect.

Zacchaeus ran! Not only that, but he also climbed a sycamore tree and hid among the leafy branches. He hoped desperately that no one would see him. That would be humiliating! Grown men *never* ran or climbed trees. But Zacchaeus *really* wanted to see Jesus.

Then Jesus did something Zacchaeus didn't expect.

Jesus walked right up to the sycamore tree, looked up, and said, "Zacchaeus, hurry up! Come down, because I'm staying at your house today."

The crowd couldn't believe it! Why did Jesus want to stay with this sinful tax collector? Didn't Jesus know what kind of man this was?

But Zacchaeus was so happy! Jesus was coming to his "unclean" house, even though he was a sinner! Zacchaeus realized how much Jesus loved him. He also realized how much he had hurt others. The tax collector promised to give back what he had stolen and to begin making things right at once. Zacchaeus believed!

Jesus announced, "Today salvation has come to this house, since he also is a son of Abraham. For the Son of Man came to seek and to save the lost" (Luke 19:9–10).

Because of Jesus, Zacchaeus was rescued and accepted. Jesus showed Zacchaeus grace and welcomed him into the family of Abraham. Zacchaeus wasn't alone anymore; he could love and be loved!

. . . .

How did Jesus change Zacchaeus's life?

The Kind Master

Matthew 20

*"'Am I not allowed to do what I choose with what belongs to me? Or do you
begrudge my generosity?' So the last will be first, and the first last."*
MATTHEW 20:15–16

Jesus told many stories to help people understand God, His kingdom, and grace. Here is one of those stories.

A vineyard owner went out early one morning to find workers. Men who needed jobs would stand in the market, waiting for someone to hire them. The master found workers and promised to pay them a denarius, a fair amount for a day's work. The men were happy to work and provide for their families.

Later that morning, the master returned to the market and found others who were standing and waiting, eagerly hoping to find work. The master hired them too.

The owner returned again at noon and once more in the afternoon. Each time he found more men in need of work, so he hired them and promised to pay them what was right.

An hour before sunset, the master returned to the market one last time and found men who had been standing and hoping and waiting *all day.* They needed money to buy food for their hungry families! The kind master saw these desperate men and hired them too.

At the end of the day, the master told his steward to pay *all* the workers. Those who had arrived last were given their money first. They were each given a denarius! They looked at the money and were so happy to take it home and buy food for their families. The master gave them what they needed, even though they hadn't earned it.

When those who had worked all day came, they expected to be paid more. But they were paid one denarius, just like those who had worked only one hour—exactly what the master had promised them that morning. That made them angry. They didn't think it was fair!

But the good and generous master gave each worker what he needed. He showed grace to those who needed much, and grace to those who needed little. Grace for everyone!

. . . .

How is Jesus like the kind master in this story?

Jesus Heals Men with Leprosy
Luke 17

Bless the LORD, O my soul, and forget not all his benefits, who forgives all your iniquity, who heals all your diseases, who redeems your life from the pit, who crowns you with steadfast love and mercy, who satisfies you with good so that your youth is renewed like the eagle's.
PSALM 103:2–5

Once, there were ten men with a skin disease called leprosy. Because of their disease, they had to leave their families and their homes and live far away. Everyone thought they were "unclean" sinners, and they weren't allowed to touch anyone or be close to anyone.

These men had heard about Jesus and His power, and then they saw Him! He was about to walk into a village, and they knew He was their only hope for being healed.

They called out in a loud voice, "Jesus, Master, have mercy on us" (Luke 17:13).

Jesus saw the poor men and loved them. He said, "Go and show yourselves to the priests" (v. 13).

Usually, only people who had been healed went to the priests. The priests would check them to make sure they were actually clean and free from disease. But Jesus had told them to go, so the ten men obeyed.

As the men were walking, something amazing happened. Suddenly, they were healed! Their skin disease was all gone! The astonished men continued on their way to see the priests, eager to be declared clean again and join their families.

But one man stopped. He had to do one thing first.

He rushed back to Jesus, crying out praises to God in a loud voice. He fell on his face at Jesus' feet and thanked this beautiful Rescuer. Jesus had made him well and given him new life! He could live in his village with his family again.

This humble, grateful man was a Samaritan.

Jesus asked, "Where are the others? The only one to return and praise God is this foreigner!" Jesus wanted people to see that He came to give new life and show mercy to *all* who believe, not just the Jews.

Jesus said to the healed man, "Rise and go your way; your faith has made you well" (v. 19).

• •

How would you feel if you had to live apart from your family?

DAY
30

The Great Banquet
Luke 14

On this mountain the Lord of hosts will make for all peoples a feast of rich food.…
He will swallow up death forever; and the Lord God will wipe away tears from all
faces.… "Behold, this is our God; we have waited for him, that he might save us."
ISAIAH 25:6, 8–9

Do you like parties? The Jewish people were waiting for a big, important party that God had promised through the prophet Isaiah long ago. Everyone wanted to be at that banquet! The Messiah would come and make everything new, wipe away everyone's tears, and invite people from all nations to celebrate!

Jesus once told a story about what this special party would be like. He told of a man who hosted a great banquet. The man made sure to have the best food and drinks. When everything was ready, he sent his servant out to tell his guests that it was time!

But when the servant went to the first guest, he had a silly excuse. He said he needed to go look at some land—that was more important than the big party. And the second person said he'd rather see how well his oxen could pull things. The third said he was busy with his new wife.

The servant was embarrassed. How could these men treat his master like this? Everything was ready! They had worked so hard to make the banquet just right!

The servant knew his master would be angry and hurt. The master *was* angry, but then he did something surprising. The master told his servant to go out into the streets and invite common people to the banquet—strangers, people who were sick and poor, and those who were blind and unable to walk.

And that's what the servant did. People who would normally never have the chance to go to a banquet like this were invited to be guests of honor! They could never repay the master. But the kind master loved these people. He turned his anger into grace.

There was still room for more, so the master sent his servant out to the highways and hedges to gather anyone who wanted to come. Everyone was invited! And God's special party will be just like this—when everything will be made new, and everyone will be welcome.

. . . .

How do you think the people at the party felt about the kind master?

Jesus Enters as King

Matthew 21; Mark 11; Luke 19; John 12

Rejoice greatly, O daughter of Zion! Shout aloud, O daughter of Jerusalem! Behold, your king is coming to you; righteous and having salvation is he, humble and mounted on a donkey.

ZECHARIAH 9:9

It was time. Jesus was entering Jerusalem, and He knew what was about to happen. He knew it was time to fulfill the promise that God made long ago to rescue His people. Jesus tried to tell His disciples what was going to happen to Him in Jerusalem, but they didn't understand. They still thought Jesus would start His kingdom the way other kings did, by fighting His enemies.

Jesus told His friends to go into the next village. There, they would find a mother donkey and her baby. Jesus told them to untie the donkeys and bring them to Him. If someone asked why they were taking the donkeys, Jesus' friends should say, "The Lord needs them" (Matthew 21:3).

So Jesus' friends went and did exactly what He said to do. They brought the donkeys to Jesus and put their cloaks on them. Then Jesus sat on the young donkey and rode into Jerusalem. He didn't ride on a strong horse like a warrior king. No, not Jesus. Instead, He rode on a small donkey like the true, humble King promised long ago by the prophets.

People saw Jesus coming into Jerusalem and remembered all the good things He had done. They remembered the words of the prophets. They knew that He was the Messiah, the King sent by God to rescue them. They spread their cloaks on the road and put tree branches down to honor Jesus. They shouted out praises, saying, "Blessed is the King who comes in the name of the Lord! Peace in heaven and glory in the highest!" (Luke 19:38).

These people believed. But the Pharisees were angry and told Jesus to make the people stop. Jesus said to them, "I tell you, if these were silent, the very stones would cry out" (v. 40).

. . . .

How do you praise and honor Jesus as King?

Jesus Clears the Temple
Matthew 21; Mark 11; Luke 19–20

*"I have said these things to you, that in me you have peace. In the world you
will have tribulation. But take heart; I have overcome the world."*
JOHN 16:33

Although many people were happy to see Jesus coming into Jerusalem, Jesus was troubled. As He looked out over the city, He knew that some people believed, but others did not. Some wanted to be rescued and made new, but others thought they were fine all by themselves. Jesus wanted peace for His people, but He knew great trouble was ahead. And Jesus cried for the people who still didn't believe.

Jesus entered the Temple, His Father's house. But He did not feel at home there that day. People were misusing the Temple. It was no longer a place for being close to God. It was more like a market!

Jewish men needed to offer animals and coins to the priests in the Temple. Money-changers traded with people to help them get the animals and coins they needed. But sometimes the money-changers were greedy and dishonest, taking more than they should and keeping the extra for themselves.

This made Jesus angry. He drove out all the buyers and sellers, turning over their tables and seats. "This is a house of prayer and worship," Jesus said. "But you are making it a den of robbers!"

When the Temple was cleared out, Jesus made room for those who knew they needed to be rescued. People who were blind and lame came to Jesus, and He healed them. Children saw what Jesus did and cried out, "Hosanna to the Son of David!" (Matthew 21:15).

The religious leaders saw these things and were so angry that they wanted to kill Jesus. They did not think Jesus had the authority to do such things. They didn't understand that Jesus would be the new Temple, the new way to heal broken friendships between God and people.

. . . .

Why did Jesus make some people leave the Temple? Who came to see Jesus at the Temple?

The Last Supper
Matthew 26; Mark 14; Luke 22; John 13

"A new commandment I give to you, that you love one another: just as I have loved you, you also are to love one another."
JOHN 13:34

It was time to celebrate Passover. Long ago, the Jewish people had been slaves in Egypt. On the night of Passover, God had told each family to pick a perfect male lamb and kill it. God had said to spread the lamb's blood on their doorway, allowing death to "pass over" that home. Everyone inside a home protected with blood was saved. That same night, Pharaoh finally set the Jewish slaves free.

Jesus and His close friends gathered to eat the Passover meal together. But as they were reclining around the table, Jesus stood up, got water and a towel, and dressed like a slave. Then He went around the room, washing His disciples' feet! Why was the Messiah, the Son of God, washing "unclean" feet? Washing feet was work for slaves, not for the King!

When it was Peter's turn, he said, "No! You can't wash *my* feet!" But Jesus told Peter that He *must* serve Peter this way. When He was finished, Jesus said, "If I then, your Lord and Teacher, have washed your feet, you also ought to wash one another's feet" (John 13:14). Jesus was showing them what true love looks like.

Jesus took bread, gave thanks, broke it, and gave it to His friends. "This is my body, which is given for you. Do this in remembrance of me" (Luke 22:19). Then Jesus took a cup of wine. "This cup that is poured out for you is the new covenant in my blood" (v. 20).

Long ago, disobedience brought evil and death into the world. But God made a covenant—a friendship promise—with His people. He would send His Son to crush evil and rescue us. Jesus' body would break and give us true life. By His blood, we would be rescued from death and set free. He would help us truly love.

Jesus, the Rescuer, would be the final sacrifice, bringing people close to God and each other forever. Through His body and blood, He offers a new covenant, taking away our sin and writing His law of love on our hearts.

• •

How did Jesus show love to His friends? How does He show love to us?

Jesus Prays
Matthew 6, 26; Mark 14; Luke 11, 22

*"The glory that you have given me I have given to them, that they may be one even
as we are one, I in them and you in me, that they may become perfectly one."*
JOHN 17:22–23

Jesus loved to pray. Sometimes He prayed with others, and sometimes He prayed alone. Jesus taught His followers how to talk with God and be close to Him.

Jesus said to pray to our Father in heaven, who is holy. Our Father loves us and wants to hear from us. He is all good with no bad in Him.

Jesus said to pray for God's kingdom to come and God's will to be done, here on earth as it is in heaven. In God's kingdom, everything is good. People love and know they are loved.

Jesus said to ask God to give us what we need each day. God is like a Good Shepherd who gives His sheep everything they need to live and grow. We can trust Him. He has provided for His people for thousands of years.

Jesus said to ask God to forgive our sins and to help us forgive others. People are selfish and hurt each other. But Jesus forgives us for the bad we do, and He shows us how to forgive others.

Jesus said to ask God to keep us away from evil things that hurt our friendship with God and each other. God will help us stay close to Him.

After Jesus ate the Passover meal with His friends, He took them to a place called Gethsemane to pray. Jesus prayed that God would bring us close to Himself and to each other again. He prayed that we would be one. But Jesus knew He would have to suffer and die for that to happen.

Jesus fell on the ground in His great sorrow. He asked God to help Him, to take away the trouble to come. But then He said, "Not my will, but yours, be done" (Luke 22:42).

When He was facing His own death and men were coming to arrest Him, Jesus took time to pray. He wanted to be close to His Father.

· ·

What would you like to pray about now?

Jesus Becomes Our Sacrifice
Matthew 26–27; Mark 14–15; Luke 22–23; John 18–19

"This is my commandment, that you love one another as I have loved you. Greater love has no one than this, that someone lay down his life for his friends."
JOHN 15:12–13

When Jesus had finished praying, He woke up His sleepy friends. "Rise and let's go. My betrayer is already here." Jesus could see a great crowd coming with swords and clubs.

Judas, who had been one of Jesus' friends, was with this crowd. They wanted to arrest Jesus of Nazareth. When Jesus said, "I am He," they all fell to the ground! Peter took out a sword to fight, and he cut off a man's ear. Jesus could have fought these enemies all on His own, but that was not God's plan. He healed the man's ear and let the crowd take Him away.

The crowd took Jesus to the high priest. They covered Jesus' face, then hit Him and spit on Him. They made fun of Him, saying, "Prophesy! Who hit you?"

Peter had entered the courtyard to stay close. But when three different people asked Peter if he knew Jesus, three times Peter lied. He was too scared to tell the truth. The third time, Jesus looked at Peter, and a rooster crowed. Jesus had warned Peter that he would deny that he knew Jesus three times. He was right! Peter was ashamed and cried very hard.

The chief priests took Jesus to their Roman leader, Pilate. Pilate wanted to set Jesus free. But the Jewish people listened to their leaders, and they said Jesus should die and the murderer Barabbas should go free instead. So Jesus, who was innocent, was crucified. He was nailed by His hands and feet to a wooden cross for everyone to see. A sign above His head said: "This is the King of the Jews" (Luke 23:38).

Two guilty men were put on crosses beside Jesus. One of them mocked Jesus, but the other man believed! This man said, "Jesus, remember me when you come into your kingdom" (v. 42). Jesus answered, "Today you will be with me in paradise" (v. 43).

On the cross, Jesus looked out at the crowds and said, "Father, forgive them, for they know not what they do" (v. 34). About noon, everything went black and the sun didn't shine. Jesus called out, "Father, into your hands I commit my spirit!" (v. 46). And then Jesus died.

. . . .

Jesus died in place of Barabbas. Who else deserves death but gets life from Jesus instead?

The Curtain Is Torn
Matthew 27; Mark 15; Luke 23; John 19

*"You shall know that I am the L*ORD*, when I open your graves, and raise
you from your graves, O my people. And I will put my Spirit within you,
and you shall live, and I will place you in your own land."*
EZEKIEL 37:13–14

When Jesus died, everything was dark, and the ground shook with an earthquake. The people watching were so sad that they beat their chests. The women who had followed Jesus stood at a distance, horrified. How could the Messiah die? Would no one else be rescued or healed? Would they never see Him again?

The Son of God died in our place so we could have life. Rocks split apart and tombs were opened. Many people buried in those tombs came back to life because of Jesus!

A Roman soldier standing by Jesus' cross saw all of this happen and suddenly realized what he had done. He and those with him were filled with wonder and said, "Truly this was the Son of God!" (Matthew 27:54). The Roman soldier believed!

Other things happened too. The curtain in the Temple was torn in two, from top to bottom. That curtain separated people from God's presence in the holiest place in the Temple. But Jesus came to bring us close to God again. Since He died in our place, nothing can separate us from God's love! Everyone can be friends with God again, like Adam and Eve were in the beginning.

An important Jewish leader named Joseph of Arimathea wanted to bury Jesus. It was dangerous to let people know that he believed in Jesus, but he had courage and asked Pilate for the body.

Nicodemus the Pharisee also believed. Nicodemus brought very expensive spices to put around Jesus' body. Nicodemus and Joseph knew they were burying the Promised Son of God. They wrapped His body with spices and cloths and placed it in an expensive tomb, sealed with a large stone.

The women who loved Jesus saw where they placed His body. The next day was the Sabbath, when they must rest, but they planned to come back the following morning.

• •

What do you think made the Roman soldier believe that Jesus was God's Promised Son?

Jesus Is Alive!

Matthew 28; Mark 16; Luke 24; John 20

"After two days he will revive us; on the third day he will raise us up, that we may live before him. Let us know; let us press on to know the LORD; his going out is sure as the dawn; he will come to us as the showers, as the spring rains that water the earth."

HOSEA 6:2–3

Early Sunday morning, Mary Magdalene, a friend of Jesus, went with some other women to Jesus' tomb. They wanted to honor Jesus by putting more spices and ointments on His body. As they walked, they wondered how they would move the heavy stone in front of the tomb.

But when they arrived, the stone had already been rolled away! They went into the tomb, but Jesus' body was gone. Suddenly two men as white as lightning appeared, and the women were terrified. The angels said, "Why do you seek the living among the dead? He is not here, but has risen" (Luke 24:5–6).

The women rushed back to tell the other disciples, but the men didn't believe them. Peter and John ran to see for themselves. It was true! Jesus' body really was gone!

They left, but Mary Magdalene stood crying outside the empty tomb. A man came and asked her why she was crying. Mary thought He was the gardener at first. But then He said her name.

Mary turned quickly. She knew that voice!

"Rabboni!" she exclaimed. Her Teacher and Rescuer was alive!

Mary went and told everyone that Jesus really was alive and was making all things new! That evening, Jesus' friends were together in a locked room when Jesus came and stood among them.

"Peace be with you," Jesus said (John 20:21). Then He breathed on them so they could receive God's Spirit. Long ago, God had breathed life into Adam, and he had walked with God. Now, Jesus breathed life into His disciples, and they would walk with God and help others do the same. Jesus had brought His friends close to God again! Because of His death, people could come close to God and each other, knowing God as their good Father.

. . . .

How did Jesus bring people close to God and to each other again?

My Lord and My God
John 20

And he said to them, "Why are you troubled, and why do doubts arise in your hearts? See my hands and my feet, that it is I myself. Touch me, and see. For a spirit does not have flesh and bones as you see that I have."

LUKE 24:38–39

The first time Jesus saw His friends in the locked room, Thomas wasn't there. Everyone else had seen Jesus' pierced hands and side. They *knew* it really was Him! But when they told Thomas about it, he didn't believe. It seemed too good to be true. Thomas said he wouldn't believe until he too saw Jesus' scars.

Eight days later, Jesus' friends were once again gathered together behind a locked door. But that didn't stop Jesus! He appeared and told them, "Peace be with you" (John 20:19).

This time Thomas was with the others. Jesus looked at Thomas and said, "Put your finger here, and see my hands; and put out your hand, and place it in my side. Do not disbelieve, but believe" (v. 27). Jesus was kind and patient, helping Thomas believe. Jesus loved Thomas.

It really was Jesus! Thomas said, "My Lord and my God!" (v. 28). Thomas believed! Jesus told him, "Blessed are those who have not seen and yet have believed" (v. 29).

The Greek word for *blessed* is *makarios*, and it means "happy right now." Not everyone gets to see Jesus like Thomas did, but God helps those people believe too. Jesus opens hearts and minds to know Him, believe, and live the lives God created us to live!

Jesus knows that all people have broken friendships with God and each other. No one is able to trust God or believe, not on our own. Like Thomas, people sometimes think that God and His kingdom are too good to be true. We may think that darkness and death and evil will last forever. But they won't! Let's remember to look for the Light and live in the hope that Jesus brings to us.

Jesus is alive! One day, He will wipe away our tears and fears forever. And then we will have peace.

· ·

What is peace? Peace is enjoying good friendships with God, with people, and with all of creation.

Feed My Sheep
John 21

"As the Father has loved me, so have I loved you. Abide in my love. If you keep my commandments, you will abide in my love.... This is my commandment, that you love one another as I have loved you."
JOHN 15:9–10, 12

One day, not long after Jesus had risen from the dead, Peter and several of his friends were fishing. They had been up all night but had caught nothing. They were tired.

Just as the first light of dawn spread across the sky, a stranger on the shore called out to them, "Children, do you have any fish?" (John 21:5).

They answered, and the man told them to cast the net on the right side of the boat. And they did. Now there were so many fish that they couldn't pull up the net! This had happened to the fishermen once before, when their Friend had said something similar. Suddenly they realized who was standing on the shore! *Jesus!*

Peter dove into the water. The others dragged the net full of fish. Jesus had already lit a charcoal fire and was cooking bread and fish. He asked the disciples to bring some of their fish too. Then Jesus said, "Come and have breakfast" (v. 12). Eating together meant that they were friends.

After breakfast, Jesus spoke with Simon Peter: "Simon, son of John, do you love me more than these?" (v. 15).

Peter answered, "Yes, Lord; you know that I love you" (v. 15).

Jesus asked Peter to feed His lambs.

Two more times Jesus asked Peter if he loved Him. Two more times Peter said yes. And two more times Jesus told Peter to care for His sheep.

When Jesus was arrested in Jerusalem, Peter had lied three times, saying he didn't know Jesus. Now Peter said he loved Jesus three times. By himself, Peter couldn't love Jesus or anyone else. But all things are possible with God!

Jesus died and came back to life to rescue Peter and help him love. Jesus loved Peter and forgave him. Peter would love not only Jesus, but also others. He would love those who were like sheep that needed the Good Shepherd.

* * *

Have you ever had a second chance to do something good? What happened?

I Am with You Always
Matthew 28; Mark 16; Luke 24; Acts 1

"As you sent me into the world, so I have sent them into the world.... I do not ask for these only, but also for those who will believe in me through their word, that they may all be one, just as you, Father, are in me, and I in you."
JOHN 17:18, 20–21

It was time for Jesus, the Promised Son, to return to His Father. He had done just what He came to do. He had died as a sacrifice—in our place—to bring people close to God and to each other again. Then He had come back to life, showing that He was stronger than anything, even death! One day, He would end evil and death forever. He would wipe away our tears and make all things new.

Jesus was leaving. But His work wasn't finished yet!

Jesus told His friends to stay in Jerusalem until God's Spirit came to be with them. Jesus wasn't leaving His friends alone. Because of Jesus, God Himself would live among His people again! Soon, they would walk with God and know Him. God's Spirit would remind them of everything Jesus had taught, and He would help them love!

Jesus told them, "But you will receive power when the Holy Spirit has come upon you, and you will be my witnesses in Jerusalem and in all Judea and Samaria, and to the end of the earth" (Acts 1:8).

Jesus was sending His friends out to do the same good things He had done! They would make things new not only for their own people in Judea, but also for their enemies in Samaria. And they wouldn't stop there! Jesus was sending them out to *the end of the earth*, because He wanted to rescue all people everywhere!

Jesus promised they wouldn't do this good work alone. "And behold, I am with you always, to the end of the age" (Matthew 28:20). God's Spirit would come to help!

After Jesus said these things, He was carried up into the sky in a cloud. Then two angels came and told Jesus' friends that one day Jesus would return.

Until then, they knew what to do!

• •

What would God's Spirit help Jesus' friends do all over the world? What can God's Spirit help you do?

The Light
An Allegory

There once was a man who lived in a cave. He had been sitting in that damp, dark cave his whole life. He had never looked up at the blue sky or smelled a sweet flower or felt the cool wind against his face. Every day he watched the wall in front of him. Sometimes a dark spot would appear. He watched it closely. *What could it be?*

He often felt sad, but he didn't know why. His stomach rumbled with hunger and his mouth was dry with thirst. Other people were in the cave, and they all watched the wall, arguing about the dark spots. A hot fire burned behind them. They didn't know it, but those dark spots were shadows.

One day, one shadow seemed to fill the whole cave. Someone new had come. The man tried to turn his head to see the visitor, but he couldn't. A fresh, sweet smell filled the man's nose. The visitor was very near. Then the man heard the Voice.

"Do you want to be free?"

"I don't know what that means," the man replied, his heart beating faster.

"It means you will get up from this dark cave, see the Light, and live the way you were created to live," answered the Voice.

"I don't think I can leave the cave." The man shut his eyes tight, tears falling.

"Do you want to be free?" repeated the Voice.

The man knew nothing but the cave and the shadows. "Who are you?" he asked.

"I am the Messiah. I am the Light and the Bread of Life. I am the Good Shepherd and the Lamb of God. I am the Son of Man and the Son of God," the Voice thundered.

The man bowed his head. Somehow, he knew this strange, thundering Voice. Somehow, it felt like a friend. The man cried out, "YES! I want to be free!"

Gentle hands unlocked the chains on the man's neck, hands, and feet. Strong arms lifted the man and carried him up, up, up out of the dark cave.

The Light was so bright! When the man could open his eyes, he saw green grass dotted with bright flowers. He felt the warm sun. He heard birds chirping and people laughing. Then he turned and looked at his Rescuer, whose smiling face shone with love and perfect joy. The man knew he would stay here, live with those laughing people, and run through the fields singing with the birds … forever. And the man was free.

"I am the LORD; I have called you in righteousness;
    I will take you by the hand and keep you;
I will give you as a covenant for the people,
    a light for the nations,
    to open the eyes that are blind,
to bring out the prisoners from the dungeon,
    from the prison those who sit in darkness."

ISAIAH 42:6–7

And now the LORD says,
    he who formed me from the womb to be his servant,
to bring Jacob back to him;
    and that Israel might be gathered to him—
for I am honored in the eyes of the LORD,
    and my God has become my strength—
he says:
"It is too light a thing that you should be my servant
    to raise up the tribes of Jacob
    and to bring back the preserved of Israel;
I will make you as a light for the nations,
    that my salvation may reach to the end of the earth."

ISAIAH 49:5–6

ACKNOWLEDGMENTS

The story behind this book is a little different from that of *The Advent Storybook*, but many of the same people came together to make it happen.

My husband, Matt, has faithfully supported our family and kept things running when I needed to retreat to my computer to write.

Laura Derico, the developmental editor, once again understood my message and skillfully distilled it down into a book easily understood by little ones.

Ian Dale, the talented illustrator, has brought to life the true story of a first-century Jewish man who came to rescue us all. Some of his illustrations made me cry, while others made me laugh. And they all reminded me of the beauty and love of Jesus, the Promised Son of God.

David C Cook bravely offered to publish this book via the traditional route, which meant we didn't need a Kickstarter campaign! I remember when Laura Derico said that her team was interested in the book, even before sales numbers came in for *The Advent Storybook*. My respect for David C Cook grew even more, because I have a feeling that publishers who care more about people than profits are rare.

A majority of these stories relied heavily on the wisdom and writings of Dr. Kenneth Bailey, a New Testament scholar and theologian who spent most of his life in the Middle East. His cultural insights and deep love for Jesus greatly enriched my understanding—and therefore writing—of these stories. If you find something new or beautiful in an otherwise familiar story, the credit almost certainly goes to him.

God did the impossible again! He turned my dream into a reality that will hopefully be enjoyed by families across the world. May we see His beauty and delight in His great love. To Him be the glory!

ABOUT THE CREATORS

Laura Richie is a wife, homeschooling mom, registered nurse, and author. A missionary kid for several years, Laura confesses she didn't truly understand her need to be rescued until later in life. Now she delights in sharing the beauty and grace of her Rescuer, especially through her books *The Advent Storybook* and *The Easter Storybook*. Laura resides in Oklahoma with her husband and children.

Ian Dale is an illustrator and designer who loves to invest in projects that share the hope and meaning that have transformed his life. He has created art for clients such as World Vision, the American Bible Society, Compassion International, and the *Bible App for Kids*, which has been enjoyed in more than thirty languages. Ian and his wife are raising their children in Los Angeles, California. Visit him online at iandale.net.

....

Watch for the story of God's kingdom to continue!

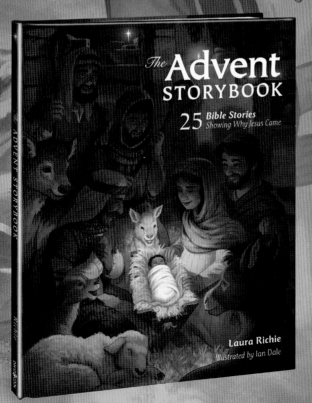